MARSHMALLOW HEAVEN

DELICIOUS, UNIQUE, AND FUN RECIPES FOR
SWEET HOMEMADE TREATS

MARSHMALLOW
HEAVEN

TRICIA M. ARCE
PHOTOGRAPHS BY JOANIE SIMON

Skyhorse Publishing

Skyhorse Publishing books may be purchased in bulk at special discounts for sales promotion, corporate gifts, fund-raising, or educational purposes. Special editions can also be created to specifications. For details, contact the Special Sales Department, Skyhorse Publishing, 307 West 36th Street, 11th Floor, New York, NY 10018 or info@ skyhorsepublishing.com.

Skyhorse® and Skyhorse Publishing® are registered trademarks of Skyhorse Publishing, Inc.®, a Delaware corporation.

Visit our website at www.skyhorsepublishing.com.

10 9 8 7 6 5 4 3 2 1

Library of Congress Cataloging-in-Publication Data is available on file.

Cover design by Jane Sheppard
Cover photo credit Joanie Simon

Print ISBN: 978-1-5107-2359-7
Ebook ISBN: 978-1-5107-2362-7

Printed in China

Dedication

To Grandmother Inez B. Ceballos

Never without you

Contents

Introduction

The one question everyone asks when they meet me and they see all the different marshmallows I can make is, "How did you come up with this?" Did I just wake up one day and think "I'm going to make marshmallow"? Or do I have some type of culinary background?

I went to school for my bachelor's degree in business management so I could climb that corporate ladder—baking or candy-making was not on the horizon. Sure, I'd baked a cookie or made the occasional cupcake, but policies and procedures were my strong suits along with customer service and people management. Then one day at work, a group of managers decided to have a fun baking competition to see which of us were better. We were a competitive group who liked to have fun, so we implemented a baking contest just like *Top Chef*. Every month, we were given a secret ingredient. The directions emailed to us for the month of February included the secret ingredient marshmallow.

I remember this month's competion because I had just lost my best friend five months prior, my grandmother, whom I had been taking care of for the past five years. Every Tuesday afternoon, we'd have a lunch date; Friday afternoons were for doctor appointments and grocery stores. Once a month was the occasional bingo date and in between were multiple daily phone calls. Unfortunately, dementia/Alzheimer's had taken her and my world stopped. My Tuesdays were now empty, my phone no longer rang, and my best friend was gone.

When that February's secret ingredient presented itself, I didn't want to just go and buy marshmallows to add to a dessert—I wanted to make an actual marshmallow. I wanted to know how a marshmallow was made. I did not own a mixer, measuring spoons, or any type of baking ingredients, so online I went to learn how to make a marshmallow. I grabbed all the tools of the trade, set up my mixer, and started adding a little of this, mixing a little bit of that, and soon I was creating my first marshmallow—strawberry flavored, very ambitious.

To my surprise, it was stickier than I thought it'd be, and doubled in volume. Ever see that scene from *Ghostbusters* when Stay Puft is blown up? That was my kitchen—pink slime everywhere including my elbows and possibly behind my ear. I was hooked, not only because it was sweet, challenging, and tasted good but because, for that moment, I felt a purpose again. I didn't know what it was going to be, but you can call it my "a-ha" moment. I had been mourning the loss of my grandmother, and for the first time, in

my kitchen, I wasn't. Instead, I was trying to figure out how to make this pink, sticky mess into a sweet dessert treat for everyone to enjoy. I truly feel this was a gift from my grandmother; I adored her, missed her terribly, felt lost, and I believe she gave this to me. I tell people that I believe it's her way of saying thank you; she gave this to me to fill that empty void, to feel as if I had a purpose. Her passing was the worst day of my life but this . . . this is the best gift I've ever been given.

Now I get to make marshmallows full time, and it's the best job ever. I get to create different flavors and desserts made of marshmallows. I left the corporate world and became an entrepreneur—something I never dreamed of happening or thought I could do. I get to say I make marshmallows for a living, how fun is that? And I've been lucky enough to build a business with my wife who is equally as creative and who understood my vision. With her knowledge of design and branding, and my marshmallow madness we opened a marshmallow shop in August 2014. Together we have created something unique and different and have been lucky to receive recognition and the ability to share our creation.

So, I wrote this book not to just have another cookbook on the bookshelves or to see my name on the cover. I really wanted to write this how-to book to hopefully inspire someone—you—to try something new. I hope you create these tasty marshmallows and memories with your loved ones or even by yourself. I hope you are just as excited as I was when they turned out delicious and terrific. I hope that excitement fuels something inside of you and pushes you to keep trying new things. I'm hoping you read through here and see that I was just an everyday nine-to-five girl in a very gray world and then, through the loss of a loved one, I stumbled upon colors. Making my first marshmallow catapulted me to want to be more, to create more, to have more of a marking in this short life we live. So with this book, I hope you find your inspiration and do the impossible just once because you never know where it might take you.

"I'd rather go broke building my dreams then just get by living somebody else's."
—Anonymous

CHAPTER 1
The 1,2,3 of Marshmallow Making

INGREDIENTS

SUGAR

Through trial and error, I have learned what sugar works best. We tried a few different sugars because 1) we wanted to be cost effective and 2) somewhat healthy. I gave up on the healthy when I realized dang it, I wanted an indulgent sweet treat, something delicious. The only sugar that is perfect for your marshmallow is pure cane sugar, and you'll need quite a bit of it. All marshmallows created through this journey have been made with pure cane sugar. We did try to use a raw sugar, and we were excited because the cost was not as high, but we quickly found out that the marshmallow I was creating with my little knowledge of the science would not produce a great outcome. Using the raw sugar, my marshmallows were extremely sticky and would not release from the pans. My own research found that sugar in the raw holds molasses, and the recipe that I use to create marshmallows does not account for the molasses. So, to keep it simple and delicious, I would recommend pure cane sugar. Any brand will do.

CORN SYRUP OR SIMPLE SYRUP

Why do we need this for marshmallows? You need something to keep the sugar from crystallizing as you cook it on the stove top. This also adds to the density and chewiness of your marshmallow. When I first started making marshmallows, I used Karo light corn syrup. Karo claims to have zero grams of high fructose in their corn syrup. Being a novice, this was the most available and simple way of making marshmallows. After a year of creating marshmallows and taking them to farmer's market's I found that I was often asked if I used corn syrup. When I would reply with yes, the customers would tell me either their family members or themselves were allergic to corn. I had to come up with an alternative solution that was available for everyone to enjoy and decided on simple syrup. Throughout this book, the measurements are the same for corn syrup and simple syrup, so use what's best for you. You can purchase simple syrup at your local grocery store unless you want to make your own (there are plenty of recipes online to do so). Full disclosure: I tried making my own simple syrup, Now, if you think marshmallows take patience, this will test you. My simple syrup kept crystalizing, and I felt as though I was just wasting product, so I purchased it at the grocery store instead.

GELATIN

This ingredient is what gives a marshmallow its texture and sponginess. You can use different types of unflavored gelatin when making marshmallows, and in the beginning, we would use Knox gelatin, which you can find in any of your grocery stores, and is very common. After a year of doing so, we encountered customers asking if our marshmallows were kosher, meaning without pork product. Considering this, we decided to start using kosher gelatin. A well-known kosher gelatin that is just bovine is Great Lakes, which is a little harder to find locally but can be purchased online. Both work the same and produce the same result, but it's just a matter of preference. So, there is a "regular marshmallow," a kosher marshmallow, and a vegetarian marshmallow, the last of which I have yet to master, but if you're interested you'll find many online recipes for

using agar-agar, which is derived from algae and vegetarian friendly. All the recipes in this book use a kosher powdered gelatin at a 250 bloom. If you purchase the gelatin in packets, you will still want to measure out the correct recipe amount.

WATER

Because marshmallows are so absorbent to flavors, you want to make sure to use filtered water instead of tap water. We only use bottled water in our recipes since our water at home and at our store location is not the tastiest.

EGG WHITES

To use or not to use, that is the question. The first recipe I used did not call for egg whites and the marshmallows came out very dense and thin, but still sweet and delicious. I just wasn't happy with the look of them, and with all the research I had done and the many marshmallows I had seen, they just didn't look amazing. I then decided to use pasteurized egg whites in my recipe and was very pleased with the look and the taste of these sweet creations.

In this book, all my recipes use egg whites, which make the marshmallow more meringue and fluffy, also known as a guimauve. If you are cautious of using egg whites, you can omit this step and still have a successful marshmallow.

VANILLA

I never realized how many types of vanilla were out there and that they all varied in taste. When I created my first marshmallow, I just purchased some imitation vanilla extract from my local store, which worked perfectly, but I wanted to up my gourmet factor. I then started to buy vanilla bean paste, which is a little thicker than an extract and tastes sweeter. You can choose Bourbon, Madagascar, or Mexican vanilla bean paste to give your marshmallows a more authentic look and taste. My preference is Mexican vanilla bean paste; I feel this is the sweetest one with a pleasant aroma and makes the marshmallows stand out in flavor.

COATING

Marshmallows are super sticky, so you'll need to coat them so that they don't stick to each other or you. Again, when I first started making marshmallows, I just used cornstarch and powdered

sugar, but then realized so many people had a corn allergy. We coat all our marshmallows using 1 cup confectioners' sugar and ½ cup tapioca starch. There is no weird aftertaste, and it works perfectly in making those cubes of sweetness not stick. Sift the two ingredients in a large bowl and use it to roll your cut marshmallows through; you can also store the leftovers in an airtight container for future use.

OILS, EXTRACTS, AND EMULSIONS

I use these to enhance the flavors of my marshmallows. Sure, we can be all-natural, but I just don't feel that it gives the flavor punch we all loved or love as children. The oils and extracts I prefer are made by Silver Cloud Estates; they seem to have a stronger taste and you can use less of the flavor to give the marshmallow their taste. These will come in 4 Fl oz. Sometimes, though, I can't find the flavor in Silver Cloud, so I'll use LorAnn's food-grade essential oils and super strength flavors in the 1 Fl oz. bottles. Also, when it comes to the emulsion, I'll use LorAnn Bakery Emulsion for certain flavors, mainly in the coconut and pumpkin recipes.

COOKING SPRAY

I always use Pam cooking spray; it seems to do the perfect job. Anytime I've deterred from this brand, the marshmallows have stuck to the pans and were not usable. You'll always want to coat your pans with the cooking spray. Using a paper towel, lightly brush the sides and bottom, then coat it with the sugar mixture mentioned prior. You can also spray your spatulas when getting ready to scrape the marshmallow after mixing so it doesn't stick much.

CHOCOLATE CANDY WAFERS

There are different candy wafers out there and you can find them locally at your craft stores or grocery stores. You can grab a bag of Wilton, Guittard, Merckens, or Alpine chocolate wafers and melt them per the direction on your bag. I prefer Merckens or Alpine; they just melt smoother for dipping. Sometimes you'll have to add some vegetable oil to make the chocolate a little more fluid.

TOOLS

When I first started out, I just went to my local grocery store and purchased a simple mixer and any measuring tools needed for making marshmallows. There is no need to get expensive or go overboard to make these delicious treats at home.

CANDY THERMOMETER

You can buy these at your local craft stores, and they're super simple to use, but they must be watched. If you're like me and when you see a shiny thing and forget what you were doing, you can purchase a digital thermometer, which costs a little more but has saved me on many pots of cooking sugar. Either one will work in helping you reach that 240-degree temperature needed for your marshmallows.

SAUCEPANS

A medium saucepan is perfect for the recipes in this book. You probably already have one in your cupboard.

MEASURING CUPS

I like using a dry measuring cup for my liquid measurements. For me, it seems

to be more accurate when making my liquid sugar for the marshmallows. I'll use a Pyrex glass measuring cup for my granulated sugar.

SPATULAS, SPOONS, AND CUTTING TOOLS

You'll want to use ones that are flexible and heatproof since you will use these to scrape hot sugar and fold marshmallow with ingredients. Also, any regular set of measuring spoons will work to make these treats. As for cutting, the best method I found was a 5-inch pizza cutter but if you can't find one locally, a long sharp knife will do the trick. Just make sure to spay it with cooking spray so that the marshmallows do not stick while cutting.

STAND MIXER
When I purchased my Sunbeam stand mixer from my local grocery store, it worked perfectly to make those occasional marshmallows. If you own just a hand mixer, that would work as well, but you might have to build a tolerance for holding it for so long. I now use a Kitchenaid 350W at home, which is amazing and I love it but again simple is good and will work just the same to make your marshmallows.

9 × 9–INCH CAKE PANS
The amount made from any of these recipes will fit perfectly into this sized cake pan. This will produce twenty-five 2 × 2–inch marshmallows when cut using a knife or a 5-inch pizza cutter. You can

also pour this into any larger pan for a thinner marshmallow if you desire. Whichever you choose, just make sure to coat it with nonstick spray and the coating mixture explained earlier on page 8.

PASTRY BAG
You'll want to use a silicon bag 18 inchs in length to make life easy. These will be needed when making some of the recipes in the book, such as Marshmallow Whip and Mallow Pies. I have used plastic 12-inch pastry bags that you can find at your local craft store as well, but they can be messy.

FOOD PROCESSOR
Some of these recipes will ask for finely chopped ingredients like cookies, caramel, or nuts.

MALLOW Q&A

Here, I'm going to try to answer any questions I might have had when I started making marshmallows and had to hunt down the answers. Hopefully some of your questions will be answered here.

WHY USE A METAL OR CERAMIC BOWL INSTEAD OF A PLASTIC BOWL FOR THE EGG WHITES?

If you have previously used the plastic bowl for anything that may have had oil or butter in it, those ingredients have left a residue. When beating the eggs, this residue will interfere with the egg whites forming into stiff peaks. The whites will just remain flat. With metal or ceramic, this will not occur.

WHAT'S STRAWBERRY EZ SQUEEZE?

Strawberry EZ Squeeze is a pie filling that you can find at your local bakery stores. I tried using strawberry jam but it just didn't give it the color or taste I wanted.

WHY DID MY CHOCOLATE SEIZE UP?

Chocolate is very temperamental. Make sure the bowl that you're melting your chocolate in or the spoon that you're stirring with does not have any water on it. Water will make chocolate seize up into a paste and will not be workable. This is the same for extracts or flavor; if they have water in the ingredients do not use them in your chocolate. Only use oil based flavors in your chocolate if you want to add some taste to your dipping.

WHY IS MY MARSHMALLOW NOT FIRMING UP?

If you have been mixing your marshmallow, it's been more than 20 minutes since you added the egg whites, and the mixture is not getting thick and sticky, a few situations may have occurred.

1. Not enough gelatin—You might want to increase the gelatin to 1⅛ ounce.
2. Too much liquid in the gelatin or in the syrup at boiling—Try the recipe again with less liquid by one quarter. Make sure all measurements of liquid are on a level countertop or table so that your numbers are accurate. Liquids in marshmallow making need to be precise.

3. Egg whites—These recipes require 2 large eggs for the egg whites. If you are using frozen egg whites or ones you purchase in a carton, you might need to adjust the egg whites to be less. Too much egg whites will give the marshmallow an airier or merengue texture.

MY MARSHMALLOWS HAVE SOME MOISTURE TO THEM/A WET LOOK TO THEM EVEN AFTER COATING. WHY?

I've come to learn this happens when you under-mix a marshmallow. With marshmallows, you must be patient—you cannot rush the process. You must let it whip for at least 15 minutes so the sugar pulls like taffy. If you pour too soon, your marshmallow will firm up but will always be wet and sticky.

MY THERMOMETER SAYS 240°F, BUT MY SUGAR LOOKS DIFFERENT. WHY?

A couple of times, my sugar overcooked or undercooked, which does not make a good marshmallow. I kept measuring out my ingredients to perfection until I read about calibrating your candy thermometer (thank you, Shauna Sever). Who knew? What I had to do was set a pot of water on the stove and place the candy thermometer in it. I had to figure out what water boils at in Arizona, where I live, and see if my thermometer reached that point within 10 minutes of the water boiling. Shauna's method is more cost effective and you can find it at shaunasever.com. I, on the other hand, just went and bought a new thermometer if it didn't reach the degree necessary.

HOW DO I KEEP MY MARSHMALLOWS SOFT AFTER CUTTING?

Air is the marshmallow's enemy. If the marshmallows hang out in the open for too long, they will start to get hard and start looking like what I call elephant ears: wrinkly. After cutting your marshmallows, place them in an airtight container. If you can, place them in a plastic ziptop bag and then in an airtight container. This will keep their freshness for up to three weeks.

CHAPTER 2

Classic Mallows

VANILLA BEAN

Place the gelatin into the bowl of a stand mixer along with ½ cup of cold water, and mix lightly to incorporate the water and gelatin. Have the whisk attachment standing by.

In a small metal or ceramic bowl, preferably not plastic, mix two egg whites till they are stiff peaks and set aside.

In a small saucepan, combine ½ cup water at room temperature, granulated sugar, simple syrup or light corn syrup, and salt. Place over medium-high heat, clip a candy thermometer (best to use a digital thermometer if you have one) onto the side of the pan, and continue to cook until the mixture reaches 240°F, approximately 7 to 8 minutes. Once the mixture reaches this temperature, immediately remove from the heat.

Turn the mixer on low speed and, while running, slowly pour the sugar syrup down the side of the bowl into the gelatin mixture. Once you have added all the syrup, increase the speed to medium and mix until gelatin is dissolved. Once dissolved, turn off mixer and add in egg whites. Turn mixer to high.

1¼ ounces kosher gelatin
½ cup cold water
2 large egg whites
½ cup room-temperature water
2 cups pure cane sugar
½ cup simple syrup or light corn syrup
¼ teaspoon salt
1 teaspoon vanilla bean paste
1 cup confectioners' sugar
½ cup tapioca flour
Oil spray

Continued on page 20

Continue to whip until the mixture becomes very thick and is lukewarm, approximately 12 to 15 minutes. Add the vanilla bean paste during the last minute of whipping. While the mixture is whipping, prepare the pan as follows.

Combine the confectioners' sugar and tapioca flour in a small bowl. Lightly spray a 9 × 9–inch metal baking pan with nonstick cooking spray. Add some sugar and tapioca mixture and move around to completely coat the bottom and sides of the pan.

When ready, pour the marshmallow mixture into the prepared pan, using a lightly oiled spatula for spreading evenly. Dust the top with some confectioners' sugar and tapioca flour. Reserve the rest for later.

Allow the marshmallows to sit uncovered for at least 6 hours and up to overnight.

Turn the marshmallows out onto a cutting board and cut into ½–inch squares using a pizza wheel sprayed with cooking spray. Once cut, lightly dust all sides of each marshmallow with the remaining mixture of confectioners' sugar and tapioca flour, using additional, if necessary. Store your marshmallows in an airtight container for up to 3 weeks.

These 1½-inch marshmallows can also be cut smaller to be placed in your hot cocoa and coffee.

CHOCOLATE

Place the gelatin into the bowl of a stand mixer along with ½ cup of cold water, and mix lightly to incorporate the water and gelatin. Have the whisk attachment standing by.

In a small stainless steel or ceramic bowl, preferably not plastic, mix two egg whites till they are stiff peaks and set aside.

In a small saucepan, combine ½ cup water at room temperature, simple syrup or light corn syrup, sugar, and salt. Place over medium-high heat, clip a candy thermometer (best to use a digital thermometer if you have one) onto the side of the pan, and continue to cook until the mixture reaches 240°F, approximately 7 to 8 minutes. Once the mixture reaches this temperature, immediately remove from the heat.

Turn the mixer on low speed and, while running, slowly pour the sugar syrup down the side of the bowl into the gelatin mixture. Once you have added all the syrup, increase the speed to medium and mix until gelatin is dissolved. Once dissolved, turn off

- 1¼ ounces kosher gelatin
- ½ cup cold water
- 2 large egg whites
- ½ cup room-temperature water
- ½ cup simple syrup or light corn syrup
- 2 cups pure cane sugar
- ¼ teaspoon salt
- 1 tablespoon cocoa powder
- 1 cup confectioners' sugar
- ½ cup tapioca flour
- 1 cup confectioners' sugar
- ½ cup tapioca powder
- Oil spray

Continued on page 22

mixer and add in egg whites. Turn mixer to high.

Continue to whip until the mixture becomes very thick and is lukewarm, approximately 12 to 15 minutes. Add the cocoa powder during the last minute of whipping. While the mixture is whipping, prepare the pan as follows.

Combine the confectioners' sugar and tapioca flour in a small bowl. Lightly spray a 9 × 9–inch metal baking pan with nonstick cooking spray. Add some sugar and tapioca mixture and move around to completely coat the bottom and sides of the pan.

When ready, pour the marshmallow mixture into the prepared pan, using a lightly oiled spatula for spreading evenly. Dust the top with some remaining sugar mixture to lightly cover. Reserve the rest for later. Allow the marshmallows to sit uncovered for at least 6 hours and up to overnight.

Turn the marshmallows out onto a cutting board and cut into 1½-inch squares using a pizza wheel sprayed with cooking spray. Once cut, lightly dust all sides of each marshmallow with the sugar mixture. Store in an airtight container for up to 3 weeks.

These 1½-inch marshmallows can also be cut smaller to be placed in your hot cocoa and coffee.

STRAWBERRY

Place the gelatin into the bowl of a stand mixer along with ½ cup of cold water. Mix lightly to incorporate the water and gelatin. Have the whisk attachment standing by.

In a small stainless steel or ceramic bowl, preferably not plastic, mix two egg whites till they are stiff peaks and set aside.

In a small saucepan, combine ½ cup water at room temperature, simple syrup or light corn syrup, sugar, and salt. Place over medium-high heat, clip a candy thermometer (best to use a digital thermometer if you have one) onto the side of the pan, and continue to cook until the mixture reaches 240°F, approximately 7 to 8 minutes. Once the mixture reaches this temperature, immediately remove from the heat.

Turn the mixer on low speed and, while running, slowly pour the sugar syrup down the side of the bowl into the gelatin mixture. Once you have added all the syrup, increase the speed to medium and mix until gelatin is dissolved. Once dissolved, turn off mixer and add in egg whites, turn mixer to high.

1¼ ounces kosher gelatin
½ cup cold water
2 large egg whites
½ cup room-temperature water
½ cup simple syrup or light corn syrup
2 cups pure cane sugar
¼ teaspoon salt
1½ tablespoons Strawberry EZ Squeeze pie filling
½ teaspoon strawberry extract
1 cup confectioners' sugar
½ cup tapioca flour
Oil spray

Continued on page 26

Continue to whip until the mixture becomes very thick and is lukewarm, approximately 12 to 15 minutes. Add the Strawberry EZ Squeeze pie filling and strawberry extract during the last minute of whipping. While the mixture is whipping, prepare the pan as follows.

Combine the confectioners' sugar and tapioca flour in a small bowl. Lightly spray a 9 × 9–inch metal baking pan with nonstick cooking spray. Add some sugar and tapioca mixture and move around to completely coat the bottom and sides of the pan.

When ready, pour the marshmallow mixture into the prepared pan, using a lightly oiled spatula for spreading evenly into the pan. Dust the top with some remaining sugar mixture to lightly cover. Reserve the rest for later. Allow the marshmallows to sit uncovered for at least 6 hours and up to overnight.

Turn the marshmallows out onto a cutting board and cut into 1½-inch squares using a pizza wheel sprayed with cooking spray. Once cut, lightly dust all sides of each marshmallow with the powdered sugar and tapioca mixture. Store in an airtight container for up to 3 weeks.

This was my first marshmallow, and I had no idea what to expect. Not only was I going to make a strawberry marshmallow, but I was going to put it on a cookie and drizzle chocolate on it. I put high expectations on myself for this dessert and the contest it was attached to, never having made a marshmallow, and this is what I decided to do? Thankfully I'm stubborn and created a dessert that won the work contest for taste and creativity. Now, I make many flavors, some more difficult than others. I love this craft.

BANANA

Place the gelatin into the bowl of a stand mixer along with ½ cup of cold water. Mix lightly to incorporate the water and gelatin. Have the whisk attachment standing by.

In a small stainless steel or ceramic bowl, preferably not plastic, mix two egg whites till they are stiff peaks and set aside.

In a small saucepan, combine ½ cup water at room temperature, simple syrup or light corn syrup, sugar, and salt. Place over medium-high heat, clip a candy thermometer (best to use a digital thermometer if you have one) onto the side of the pan, and continue to cook until the mixture reaches 240°F, approximately 7 to 8 minutes. Once the mixture reaches this temperature, immediately remove from the heat.

Turn the mixer on low speed and, while running, slowly pour the sugar syrup down the side of the bowl into the gelatin mixture. Once you have added all of the syrup, increase the speed to medium and mix until gelatin is dissolved. Once dissolved, turn off mixer and add in egg whites. Turn mixer to high.

1¼ ounces kosher gelatin
½ cup cold water
2 large egg whites
½ cup room-temperature water
½ cup simple syrup or light corn syrup
2 cups pure cane sugar
¼ teaspoon salt
1 teaspoon banana extract
2 drops yellow food coloring
1 cup confectioners' sugar
½ cup tapioca flour
Oil spray

Continued on page 28

Continue to whip until the mixture becomes very thick and is lukewarm, approximately 12 to 15 minutes. Add the banana extract and yellow food coloring during the last minute of whipping. While the mixture is whipping, prepare the pan as follows.

Combine the confectioners' sugar and tapioca flour in a small bowl. Lightly spray a 9 × 9–inch metal baking pan with nonstick cooking spray. Add some sugar and tapioca mixture and move around to completely coat the bottom and sides of the pan.

When ready, pour the marshmallow mixture into the prepared pan, using a lightly oiled spatula for spreading evenly. Dust the top with some remaining sugar mixture to lightly cover. Reserve the rest for later. Allow the marshmallows to sit uncovered for at least 6 hours and up to overnight.

Turn the marshmallows out onto a cutting board and cut into 1½-inch squares using a pizza wheel sprayed with cooking spray. Once cut, lightly dust all sides of each marshmallow with the sugar mixture. Store in an airtight container for up to 3 weeks.

What do you do with Banana Marshmallows? Make a perfect s'more, of course; toast these marshmallows and place some peanut butter and chocolate on your graham crackers and you now have a peanut butter and banana s'more. What about banana marshmallows over your sweet potatoes for the holidays? Now that's something to come home to.

CHERRY

Place the gelatin and the Kool-Aid into the bowl of a stand mixer along with ½ cup of cold water. Mix lightly to incorporate the water, Kool-Aid, and gelatin. Have the whisk attachment standing by.

In a small stainless steel or ceramic bowl, preferably not plastic, mix two egg whites till they are stiff peaks and set aside.

In a small saucepan, combine ½ cup water at room temperature, simple syrup or light corn syrup, sugar, and salt. Place over medium-high heat, clip a candy thermometer (best to use a digital thermometer if you have one) onto the side of the pan, and continue to cook until the mixture reaches 240°F, approximately 7 to 8 minutes. Once the mixture reaches this temperature, immediately remove from the heat.

Turn the mixer on low speed and, while running, slowly pour the sugar syrup down the side of the bowl into the gelatin mixture. Once you have added all the syrup, increase the speed to medium and mix until gelatin is dissolved. Once dissolved, turn off mixer and add in egg whites. Turn mixer to high.

1¼ ounces of kosher gelatin
1 packet of unsweetened cherry Kool-Aid
½ cup cold water
2 large egg whites
½ cup room-temperature water
½ cup simple syrup or light corn syrup
2 cups pure cane sugar
¼ teaspoon salt
1 cup confectioners' sugar
½ cup tapioca flour
Oil spray

Continued on page 32

Continue to whip until the mixture becomes very thick and is lukewarm, approximately 12 to 15 minutes. While the mixture is whipping prepare the pan as follows.

Combine the confectioners' sugar and tapioca flour in a small bowl. Lightly spray a 9 × 9–inch metal baking pan with nonstick cooking spray. Add some sugar and tapioca mixture and move around to completely coat the bottom and sides of the pan.

When ready, pour the marshmallow mixture into the prepared pan, using a lightly oiled spatula for spreading evenly into the pan. Dust the top with enough remaining sugar mixture to lightly cover. Reserve the rest for later. Allow the marshmallows to sit uncovered for at least 6 hours and up to overnight.

Turn the marshmallows out onto a cutting board and cut into 1½-inch squares using a pizza wheel sprayed with cooking spray. Once cut, lightly dust all sides of each marshmallow with the sugar mixture. Store in an airtight container for up to 3 weeks.

This marshmallow is fun to make because you can use any type of unsweetened flavor drink mix. This marshmallow sort of reminds me of Laffy Taffy with its sweet and tart taste. We have made many flavors using unsweetened flavor drink mixes. So, although it says cherry, try grape, watermelon, or even peach mango. Just know you will have a little tartness in your mallow.

CHAPTER 3

Kid-Approved Mallows

BIRTHDAY CAKE

Place the gelatin into the bowl of a stand mixer along with ½ cup of cold water. Mix lightly to incorporate the water and gelatin. Have the whisk attachment standing by.

In a small metal or ceramic bowl, preferably not plastic, mix two egg whites till they are stiff peaks and set aside.

In a small saucepan, combine ½ cup water at room temperature, simple syrup or light corn syrup, sugar, and salt. Place over medium-high heat, clip a candy thermometer (best to use a digital thermometer if you have one) onto the side of the pan, and continue to cook until the mixture reaches 240°F, approximately 7 to 8 minutes. Once the mixture reaches this temperature, immediately remove from the heat.

Turn the mixer on low speed and, while running, slowly pour the sugar syrup down the side of the bowl into the gelatin mixture. Once you have added all the syrup, increase the speed to medium and mix until gelatin is dissolved. Once dissolved, turn off mixer and add in egg whites. Turn mixer to high.

1¼ ounce kosher gelatin
½ cup cold water
2 large egg whites
½ cup room-temperature water
½ cup simple syrup or light corn syrup
2 cups pure cane sugar
¼ teaspoon salt
1 teaspoon vanilla bean paste
1 cup confectioners' sugar
½ cup tapioca flour
½ cup gluten-free birthday cake mix
1 cup candy sprinkles
Oil spray

Continued on page 35

Continue to whip until the mixture becomes very thick and is lukewarm, approximately 12 to 15 minutes. Add the vanilla bean paste during the last minute of whipping. While the mixture is whipping, prepare the pan as follows.

Combine the confectioners' sugar and tapioca flour in a small bowl. Lightly spray a 9 × 9–inch metal baking pan with nonstick cooking spray. Add some sugar and tapioca mixture and move around to completely coat the bottom and sides of the pan.

When ready, before pouring the marshmallow mixture into the prepared pan, lightly sprinkle the cake mix on top of the marshmallow using a hand sifter along with some of the sprinkles. Fold lightly and then pour half of the marshmallow using a lightly oiled spatula for spreading evenly into the pan. With the other half of the marshmallow, repeat from above: lightly sprinkle the cake mix and a handful of sprinkles. Lightly fold and pour the rest into the pan. Once the marshmallow is evenly spread, sprinkle the remaining candy sprinkles on top and dust the top with some confectioners' sugar and tapioca flour. Reserve the rest for later. Allow the marshmallows to sit uncovered for at least 6 hours and up to overnight.

Turn the marshmallows out onto a cutting board and cut into 1½-inch squares using a pizza wheel sprayed with cooking spray. Once cut, lightly dust all sides of each marshmallow with the remaining mixture of confectioners' sugar and tapioca flour, using additional if necessary. Store in an airtight container for up to 3 weeks.

If anyone says "birthday cake," I'm the first one in line. I love birthday cake cupcakes or the smell of birthday cake candles, so why not a birthday cake marshmallow? You can basically use any cake mix for this recipe, but I use a gluten-free cake mix to appeal to everyone. Pillsbury makes one that is perfect for these little cubes of sweetness. Funny story: the first time I made them, I had the mixer going, the marshmallow looking fluffy and sticky, and was just about done so I decided to add in the cake mix. Pure novice here, following no direction I added 2 tablespoons of cake mix into the bowl only to watch a fluffy, tasty marshmallow deflate to nothing, and leave a gooey mess. WHAT HAPPENED? Staring into the bowl, frustrated, I decided to try again. This time instead of just putting the cake mix straight into the mixer I folded the cake mix in the mallow before pouring but making sure not to overmix. The second attempt, I just sprinkled a teaspoon using the hand-held sifter on top of the finished marshmallow and folded it in the marshmallow. This seemed to work perfectly. The marshmallow didn't deflate, it didn't turn into a gooey mess, and it stayed fluffy. Then added some sprinkles and boom—a perfect birthday fluff to enjoy. Because cake mix has oil in the dry mix, once it is combined into the fluffy marshmallow, the oil starts breaking down the sugar. This is why we fold and dust instead of adding the mix right into the mixing bowl.

COTTON CANDY

Place the gelatin into the bowl of a stand mixer along with ½ cup of cold water, and mix lightly to incorporate the water and gelatin. Have the whisk attachment standing by.

In a small stainless steel or ceramic bowl, preferably not plastic, mix two egg whites till they are stiff peaks and set aside.

In a small saucepan, combine ½ cup water at room temperature, simple syrup or light corn syrup, sugar, and salt. Place over medium-high heat, clip a candy thermometer (best to use a digital thermometer if you have one) onto the side of the pan, and continue to cook until the mixture reaches 240°F, approximately 7 to 8 minutes. Once the mixture reaches this temperature, immediately remove from the heat.

Turn the mixer on low speed and, while running, slowly pour the sugar syrup down the side of the bowl into the gelatin mixture. Once you have added all the syrup, increase the speed to medium and mix until gelatin is dissolved. Once dissolved, turn off mixer and add in egg whites. Turn mixer to high.

1¼ ounces kosher gelatin
½ cup cold water
2 large egg whites
½ cup room-temperature water
½ cup simple syrup or light corn syrup
2 cups pure cane sugar
¼ teaspoon salt
1 teaspoon cotton candy extract
1 cup confectioners' sugar
½ cup tapioca flour
Oil spray
blue food coloring
pink food coloring

Continued on page 40

Continue to whip until the mixture becomes very thick and is lukewarm, approximately 12 to 15 minutes. Add the cotton candy extract during the last minute of whipping. While the mixture is whipping, prepare the pan as follows.

Combine the confectioners' sugar and tapioca flour in a small bowl. Lightly spray a 9 × 9–inch metal baking pan with nonstick cooking spray. Add some sugar and tapioca mixture and move around to completely coat the bottom and sides of the pan.

When ready, pour the marshmallow mixture into the prepared pan using a lightly oiled spatula, which is used for spreading the marshmallow evenly into the pan. Place a drop of pink food coloring on one side of the spatula and on the opposite side place a blue drop of food coloring. When pouring the mix into the pan, slightly mix the colors into the marshmallow mix, giving it a rainbow effect. Dust the top with enough of the remaining powdered sugar mixture to lightly cover. Reserve the rest for later. Allow the marshmallows to sit uncovered for at least 6 hours and up to overnight.

Turn the marshmallows out onto a cutting board and cut into 1½-inch squares using a pizza wheel sprayed with cooking spray. Once cut, lightly dust all sides of each marshmallow with the sugar mixture. Store in an airtight container for up to 3 weeks.

COOKIES AND CREAM

Place the gelatin into the bowl of a stand mixer along with ½ cup of cold water; mix lightly to incorporate the water and gelatin. Have the whisk attachment standing by.

In a small stainless steel or ceramic bowl, preferably not plastic, mix two egg whites till they are stiff peaks and set aside.

In a small saucepan combine ½ cup water at room temperature, simple syrup or light corn syrup, granulated sugar, and salt. Place over medium high heat, clip a candy thermometer (best to use a digital thermometer if you have one) onto the side of the pan, and continue to cook until the mixture reaches 240°F, approximately 7 to 8 minutes. Once the mixture reaches this temperature, immediately remove from the heat.

Turn the mixer on low speed and, while running, slowly pour the sugar syrup down the side of the bowl into the gelatin mixture. Once you have added all the syrup, increase the speed to medium and mix until gelatin is dissolved. Once dissolved, turn off mixer and add in egg whites; turn mixer to high.

1¼ ounces kosher gelatin
½ cup cold water
2 large egg whites
½ cup room-temperature water
½ cup simple syrup or light corn syrup
2 cups of pure cane sugar
¼ teaspoon salt
1 teaspoon vanilla bean paste
Confectioners' sugar
Tapioca flour
2 cups finely crushed Oreo cookies
½ cup broken Oreo cookies
Oil spray

Continued on page 42

Continue to whip until the mixture becomes very thick and is lukewarm, approximately 12 to 15 minutes. Add the vanilla bean paste during the last minute of whipping. While the mixture is whipping, prepare the pan as follows.

Combine the confectioners' sugar and tapioca flour in a small bowl. Lightly spray a 9 × 9–inch metal baking pan with nonstick cooking spray. Add the sugar and tapioca mixture and move around to completely coat the bottom and sides of the pan. Then sprinkle ¼ cup of the finely ground Oreo cookie on the bottom of the pan and place the remainder to the side.

When done whipping, take off the stand and pour in the ½ cup of broken cookies into mixture and fold in. Then pour into pan using a lightly oiled spatula. Dust the top with more of the finely ground cookie. Reserve the rest for later. Allow the marshmallows to sit uncovered for at least 6 hours and up to overnight.

Turn the marshmallows out onto a cutting board and cut into 1½-inch squares using a pizza wheel sprayed with cooking spray. Once cut, lightly dust all sides of each marshmallow with the remaining finely ground Oreo cookie. Store in an airtight container for up to 3 weeks.

Being an entrepreneur is not an easy task. Some days, I just say aloud "All I wanted to do was make marshmallows!" The smiles on people's faces when they bite into a marshmallow or when they smell it being toasted—that is the reason I wake up and get to the kitchen and create new flavors. I never thought being an entrepreneur was in my path but here it is. There is no guidebook on how to be successful, but my passion for making marsh-mallows drives me to figure it out. If you believe in a craft or have passion for an outcome, you wake up every morning to fight for it. I used to work fifty-five hours a week in retail and dreaded it, but it was a way to pay the bills. It was very robotic. Now I work eighty-plus hours and love it because what I do, what I create, makes people smile and creates memories. I'm going to be part of someone's story about handmade gourmet marshmallows. I want to be that woman that another woman sees and says, "She did it so I can do it too." I want a kid to come to my store location and think anything is possible. I might be a niche, but I had the want to see it happen and the determination to make it a reality.

PINK BUBBLEGUM

Place the gelatin into the bowl of a stand mixer along with ½ cup of cold water, and mix lightly to incorporate the water and gelatin. Have the whisk attachment standing by.

In a small stainless steel or ceramic bowl, preferably not plastic, mix two egg whites till they are stiff peaks and set aside.

In a small saucepan, combine ½ cup water at room temperature, simple syrup or light corn syrup, sugar, and salt. Place over medium-high heat, clip a candy thermometer (best to use a digital thermometer if you have one) onto the side of the pan, and continue to cook until the mixture reaches 240°F, approximately 7 to 8 minutes. Once the mixture reaches this temperature, immediately remove from the heat.

Turn the mixer on low speed and, while running, slowly pour the sugar syrup down the side of the bowl into the gelatin mixture. Once you have added all of the syrup, increase the speed to medium and mix until gelatin is dissolved. Once dissolved, turn off mixer and add in egg whites. Turn mixer to high.

1¼ ounces kosher gelatin
½ cup cold water
2 large egg whites
½ cup room-temperature water
½ cup simple syrup or light corn syrup
2 cups pure cane sugar
¼ teaspoon salt
1 teaspoon bubblegum extract
3 drops pink food coloring
1 cup confectioners' sugar
½ cup tapioca flour
Oil spray

Continued on page 46

Continue to whip until the mixture becomes very thick and is lukewarm, approximately 12 to 15 minutes. Add the bubble gum extract and food coloring during the last minute of whipping. While the mixture is whipping, prepare the pan as follows.

Combine the confectioners' sugar and tapioca flour in a small bowl. Lightly spray a 9 × 9–inch metal baking pan with nonstick cooking spray. Add some sugar and tapioca mixture and move around to completely coat the bottom and sides of the pan.

When ready, pour the marshmallow mixture into the prepared pan using a lightly oiled spatula, which is used for spreading the marshmallow evenly. Dust the top with enough of the remaining powdered sugar mixture to lightly cover. Reserve the rest for later. Allow the marshmallows to sit uncovered for at least 6 hours and up to overnight.

Turn the marshmallows out onto a cutting board and cut into 1½-inch squares using a pizza wheel sprayed with cooking spray. Once cut, lightly dust all sides of each marshmallow with the sugar mixture. Store in an airtight container for up to 3 weeks.

FRUITY CEREAL

Place the gelatin into the bowl of a stand mixer along with ½ cup of cold water, and mix lightly to incorporate the water and gelatin. Have the whisk attachment standing by.

In a small stainless steel or ceramic bowl, preferably not plastic, mix two egg whites till they are stiff peaks and set aside.

In a small saucepan, combine ½ cup water at room temperature, simple syrup or light corn syrup, sugar, and salt. Place over medium-high heat, clip a candy thermometer (best to use a digital thermometer if you have one) onto the side of the pan, and continue to cook until the mixture reaches 240°F, approximately 7 to 8 minutes. Once the mixture reaches this temperature, immediately remove from the heat.

Turn the mixer on low speed and, while running, slowly pour the sugar syrup down the side of the bowl into the gelatin mixture. Once you have added all of the syrup, increase the speed to medium and mix until gelatin is dissolved. Once dissolved, turn off mixer and add in egg whites; turn mixer to high.

- 1¼ ounce kosher gelatin
- ½ cup cold water
- 2 large egg whites
- ½ cup room-temperature water
- ½ cup simple syrup or light corn syrup
- 2 cups of pure cane sugar
- ¼ teaspoon salt
- 1 teaspoon vanilla bean paste
- 1 cup fruity cereal
- 10 golden cookies
- Oil spray
- 1 cup confectioners' sugar

Continued on page 48

Continue to whip until the mixture becomes very thick and is lukewarm, approximately 12 to 15 minutes. Add the vanilla bean paste during the last minute of whipping.

You will want to use a food processor to finely grind up the cereal with the cookies. This mixture will coat the marshmallows.

While the mixture is whipping, prepare the pan as follows.

Lightly spray a 9 × 9–inch metal baking pan with nonstick cooking spray. Place the confectioners' sugar in pan and move around to completely coat the bottom and sides of the pan. Then, with ¼ cup of the cereal mix, sprinkle the bottom of pan.

When ready, pour the marshmallow mixture into the prepared pan using a lightly oiled spatula, which is used for spreading the marshmallow evenly. While pouring, fold in ½ a cup of the cereal mixture. Dust the top with some of the remaining cereal mixture. Reserve the rest for later. Allow the marshmallows to sit uncovered for at least 6 hours and up to overnight.

Turn the marshmallows out onto a cutting board and cut into 1½–inch squares using a pizza wheel sprayed with cooking spray. Once cut, lightly dust all sides of each marshmallow with the cereal mixture. Store in an airtight container for up to 3 weeks.

STRAWBERRY BANANA

Place the gelatin into the bowl of a stand mixer along with ½ cup of cold water, and mix lightly to incorporate the water and gelatin. Have the whisk attachment standing by.

In a small stainless steel or ceramic bowl, preferably not plastic, mix two egg whites till they are stiff peaks and set aside.

In a small saucepan, combine ½ cup water at room temperature, simple syrup or light corn syrup, sugar, and salt. Place over medium-high heat, clip a candy thermometer (best to use a digital thermometer if you have one) onto the side of the pan, and continue to cook until the mixture reaches 240°F, approximately 7 to 8 minutes. Once the mixture reaches this temperature, immediately remove from the heat.

Turn the mixer on low speed and, while running, slowly pour the sugar syrup down the side of the bowl into the gelatin mixture. Once you have added all of the syrup, increase the speed to medium and mix until gelatin is dissolved. Once dissolved, turn off mixer and add in egg whites. Turn mixer to high.

1¼ ounces kosher gelatin
½ cup cold water
2 large egg whites
½ cup room-temperature water
½ cup simple syrup or light corn syrup
2 cups pure cane sugar
¼ teaspoon salt
1 teaspoon banana extract
1 drop yellow food coloring
1 teaspoon strawberry extract
1 teaspoon Strawberry EZ Squeeze pie filling
1 cup confectioners' sugar
½ cup tapioca flour
Oil spray

Note: You will need two mixers for this marshmallow, and don't forget your 9 × 9–inch pan!

Continued on page 52

Once egg has been added, let mix for 5 minutes. You don't want this marshmallow to get to firm since you must divide between two mixers. After five minutes, pour half of the marshmallow mix into the second mixer and turn both mixers to medium speed.

Continue to whip until the mixtures becomes very thick and lukewarm, approximately 10 minutes. In that last minute, in mixer one you will add the banana extract and yellow food color, in the second mixer you will add the strawberry extract and EZ Squeeze pie filling and continue mixing. While the mixture is whipping, prepare the pan as follows.

Combine the confectioners' sugar and tapioca flour in a small bowl. Lightly spray a 9 × 9–inch metal baking pan with nonstick cooking spray. Add the some and tapioca mixture and move around to completely coat the bottom and sides of the pan.

When ready, pour the banana marshmallow mixture into the prepared pan using a lightly oiled spatula, which is used for spreading the marshmallow evenly. Once spread, then take the strawberry marshmallow and repeat over the banana flavor. Dust the top with enough of the remaining powdered sugar mixture to lightly cover. Reserve the rest for later. Allow the marshmallows to sit uncovered for at least 6 hours and up to overnight.

Turn the marshmallows out onto a cutting board and cut into 1½–inch squares using a pizza wheel sprayed with cooking spray. Once cut, lightly dust all sides of each marshmallow with the sugar mixture. Store in an airtight container for up to 3 weeks.

CHAPTER 4

Holiday Mallows

PEPPERMINT

Place the gelatin into the bowl of a stand mixer along with ½ cup of cold water, and mix lightly to incorporate the water and gelatin. Have the whisk attachment standing by.

In a small metal or ceramic bowl, preferably not plastic, mix one egg white till it forms stiff peaks and set aside.

In a small saucepan, combine ½ cup water at room temperature, sugar, simple syrup or light corn syrup, and salt. Place over medium-high heat, clip a candy thermometer (best to use a digital thermometer if you have one) onto the side of the pan, and continue to cook until the mixture reaches 240°F, approximately 7 to 8 minutes. Once the mixture reaches this temperature, immediately remove from the heat.

Turn the mixer on low speed and, while running, slowly pour the sugar syrup down the side of the bowl into the gelatin mixture. Once you have added all the syrup, increase the speed to medium and mix until gelatin is dissolved. Once dissolved, turn off mixer and add in egg white. Turn mixer to high.

Continue to whip until the mixture becomes very thick and is lukewarm,

1¼ ounces kosher gelatin
½ cup cold water
1 large egg white
½ cup room-temperature water
2 cups pure cane sugar
½ cup simple syrup or light corn syrup
¼ teaspoon salt
½ teaspoon peppermint oil
1 cup confectioners' sugar
½ cup tapioca flour
Oil spray
1 cup crushed soft pillow mints

Continued on page 58

approximately 12 to 15 minutes. Add the peppermint oil during the last minute of whipping. While the mixture is whipping, prepare the pan as follows.

Combine the confectioners' sugar and tapioca flour in a small bowl. Lightly spray a 9 × 9–inch metal baking pan with nonstick cooking spray. Add some sugar and tapioca mixture and move around to completely coat the bottom and sides of the pan.

When ready, before pouring the marshmallow mixture into the prepared pan, lightly sprinkle ¼ cup of the crushed pillow mints on top of the marshmallow mix. Fold lightly and pour half using a lightly oiled spatula. Sprinkle another ¼ cup of mints and pour in the rest of the marshmallow; once the marshmallow is evenly spread, sprinkle the rest of the pillow mints on top and dust the top with enough of the confectioners' sugar and tapioca flour mixture to cover.

Reserve the rest of the mix for later. Allow the marshmallows to sit uncovered for at least 6 hours and up to overnight.

Turn the marshmallows out onto a cutting board and cut into 1½–inch squares using a pizza wheel coated with cooking spray. Once cut, lightly dust all sides of each marshmallow with the remaining mixture of confectioners' sugar and tapioca flour, using additional if necessary. Store in an airtight container for up to 3 weeks.

These make for perfect gifts for the holidays! For an added bonus, dip half of the marshmallow into dark chocolate and let them dry a couple of minutes. These are also perfect to cut up and plop into your coffee or hot cocoa.

EGGNOG

Place the gelatin into the bowl of a stand mixer along with ½ cup of cold water, and mix lightly to incorporate the water and gelatin. Have the whisk attachment standing by.

In a small metal or ceramic bowl, preferably not plastic, mix two egg whites till they are stiff peaks and set aside.

In a small saucepan, combine ½ cup water at room temperature, sugar, simple syrup or light corn syrup, and salt. Place over medium-high heat, clip a candy thermometer (best to use a digital thermometer if you have one) onto the side of the pan, and continue to cook until the mixture reaches 240°F, approximately 7 to 8 minutes. Once the mixture reaches this temperature, immediately remove from the heat.

Turn the mixer on low speed and, while running, slowly pour the sugar syrup down the side of the bowl into the gelatin mixture. Once you have added all the syrup, increase the speed to medium and mix until gelatin is dissolved. Once dissolved, turn off mixer and add in egg whites. Turn mixer to high.

1¼ ounces kosher gelatin
½ cup cold water
2 large egg whites
½ cup room-temperature water
2 cups pure cane sugar
½ cup simple syrup or light corn syrup
¼ teaspoon salt
1 teaspoon eggnog extract
1 teaspoon rum extract
¼ teaspoon nutmeg
1 cup confectioners' sugar
½ cup tapioca flour
Oil spray

Continued on page 60

Continue to whip until the mixture becomes very thick and is lukewarm, approximately 12 to 15 minutes. Add the eggnog, rum, and nutmeg during the last minute of whipping. While the mixture is whipping, prepare the pan as follows.

Combine the confectioners' sugar and tapioca flour in a small bowl. Lightly spray a 9 × 9–inch metal baking pan with nonstick cooking spray. Add some sugar and tapioca mixture and move around to completely coat the bottom and sides of the pan.

When ready, pour mixture into pan using a lightly oiled spatula.

Once the marshmallow is evenly spread, dust the top with some of the confectioners' sugar and tapioca flour mixture. Reserve the rest for later. Allow the marshmallows to sit uncovered for at least 6 hours or overnight.

Turn the marshmallows out onto a cutting board and cut into 1½–inch squares using a pizza wheel coated with cooking spray. Once cut, lightly dust all sides of each marshmallow with the remaining mixture of confectioners' sugar and tapioca flour, using additional if necessary. Store in an airtight container for up to 3 weeks.

PUMPKIN SPICE

Place the gelatin into the bowl of a stand mixer along with ½ cup of cold water, and mix lightly to incorporate the water and gelatin. Have the whisk attachment standing by.

In a small metal or ceramic bowl, preferably not plastic, mix two egg whites till they are stiff peaks and set aside.

In a small saucepan, combine ½ cup water at room temperature, sugar, simple syrup or light corn syrup, and salt. Place over medium-high heat, clip a candy thermometer (best to use a digital thermometer if you have one) onto the side of the pan, and continue to cook until the mixture reaches 240°F, approximately 7 to 8 minutes. Once the mixture reaches this temperature, immediately remove from the heat.

Turn the mixer on low speed and, while running, slowly pour the sugar syrup down the side of the bowl into the gelatin mixture. Once you have added all the syrup, increase the speed to medium and mix until gelatin is dissolved. Once dissolved, turn off mixer and add in egg whites. Turn mixer to high.

1¼ ounces kosher gelatin
½ cup cold water
2 large egg whites
½ cup room-temperature water
2 cups pure cane sugar
½ cup simple syrup or light corn syrup
¼ teaspoon salt
1 tablespoon pumpkin puree
1 teaspoon pumpkin extract
½ teaspoon pumpkin spice
½ cup confectioners' sugar
¼ cup tapioca flour
1 cup crushed graham crackers
Oil spray

Continued on page 64

Continue to whip until the mixture becomes very thick and is lukewarm, approximately 12 to 15 minutes. Add the pumpkin purée, pumpkin extract, and pumpkin spice during the last minute of whipping. While the mixture is whipping, prepare the pan as follows.

Combine the confectioners' sugar and tapioca flour in a small bowl. Lightly spray a 9 × 9–inch metal baking pan with nonstick cooking spray. Add the sugar and tapioca mixture and move around to completely coat the bottom and sides of the pan. On the bottom of the pan, sprinkle about a ¼ cup of the crushed graham crackers and place the rest to the side.

When ready, pour the marshmallow using a lightly oiled spatula. Once the marshmallow is evenly spread, sprinkle another ¼ cup of crushed graham cracker on top. Reserve the rest for later. Allow the marshmallows to sit uncovered for at least 6 hours and up to overnight.

Turn the marshmallows out onto a cutting board and cut into 1½–inch squares using a pizza wheel coated with cooking spray. Once cut, lightly dust all sides of each marshmallow with the remaining crushed graham crackers, using additional if necessary. Store in an airtight container for up to 3 weeks.

CARAMEL APPLE

Place the gelatin into the bowl of a stand mixer along with ½ cup of cold apple juice and mix lightly to incorporate the apple juice and gelatin. Have the whisk attachment standing by.

In a small metal or ceramic bowl, preferably not plastic, mix two egg whites till they are stiff peaks and set aside.

In a small saucepan, combine ½ cup water at room temperature, sugar, simple syrup or light corn syrup, and salt. Place over medium-high heat, clip a candy thermometer (best to use a digital thermometer if you have one) onto the side of the pan, and continue to cook until the mixture reaches 240°F, approximately 7 to 8 minutes. Once the mixture reaches this temperature, immediately remove from the heat.

Turn the mixer on low speed and, while running, slowly pour the sugar syrup down the side of the bowl into the gelatin mixture. Once you have added all the syrup, increase the speed to medium and mix until gelatin is dissolved. Once dissolved, turn off mixer and add in egg whites. Turn mixer to high.

Continue to whip until the mixture becomes very thick and is lukewarm,

1¼ ounce kosher gelatin
½ cup cold apple juice
2 large egg whites
½ cup room-temperature water
2 cups pure cane sugar
½ cup simple syrup or light corn syrup
¼ teaspoon salt
1 teaspoon apple pie spice
1 teaspoon apple extract
1 cup confectioners' sugar
½ cup tapioca flour
1 cup caramel bits
Oil spray

Continued on page 66

approximately 12 to 15 minutes. In the last minute of mixing, add in apple pie spice and apple extract. While the mixture is whipping, prepare the pan as follows.

Combine the confectioners' sugar and tapioca flour in a small bowl. Lightly spray a 9 × 9–inch metal baking pan with nonstick cooking spray. Add some sugar and tapioca mixture and move around to completely coat the bottom and sides of the pan.

For the caramel bits, pour them into a food processor and grind to a medium course. Place them into a bowl to be added to the marshmallow mix.

Take half of the caramel pieces and fold into the marshmallow then pour. Once marshmallow is poured into the pan and evened out, drizzle the rest of the caramel bits over the marshmallow. Then dust the top with some confectioners' sugar and tapioca flour. Reserve the rest for later. Allow the marshmallows to sit uncovered for at least 6 hours and up to overnight.

Turn the marshmallows out onto a cutting board and cut into 1½–inch squares using a pizza wheel coated with cooking spray. Once cut, lightly dust all sides of each marshmallow with the remaining mixture of confectioners' sugar and tapioca flour, using additional if necessary. Store in an airtight container for up to 3 weeks.

I wanted something festive for the holidays, especially Halloween, so I thought the caramel apple would be great as a holiday marshmallow. Who doesn't love caramel apples? Make sure to use an all-natural juice with no sugar added; too much sugar can make the marshmallow too sticky. As for the apple pie spice, you can pick this up at any of your grocery stores. It literally says "Apple Pie Spice" on the label, which was enough for me. Caramel Apple reminds me of fall and the state fair, of being young and jumping into a pile of leaves. These little marshmallow fluffs will make for a perfect s'more; just toast it over an open fire and bite into warm caramel apple.

MEXICAN HOT CHOCOLATE

Place the gelatin into the bowl of a stand mixer along with ½ cup of cold water, and mix lightly to incorporate the water and gelatin. Have the whisk attachment standing by.

In a small metal or ceramic bowl, preferably not plastic, mix two egg whites till they are stiff peaks and set aside.

In a small saucepan, combine ½ cup water at room temperature, sugar, simple syrup or light corn syrup, and salt. Place over medium-high heat, clip a candy thermometer (best to use a digital thermometer if you have one) onto the side of the pan, and continue to cook until the mixture reaches 240°F, approximately 7 to 8 minutes. Once the mixture reaches this temperature, immediately remove from the heat.

Turn the mixer on low speed and, while running, slowly pour the sugar syrup down the side of the bowl into the gelatin mixture. Once you have added all the syrup, increase the speed to medium and mix until gelatin is dissolved. Once dissolved, turn off mixer and add in egg whites. Turn mixer to high.

1¼ ounces kosher gelatin
½ cup cold water
2 large egg whites
½ cup room-temperature water
2 cups pure cane sugar
½ cup simple syrup or light corn syrup
¼ teaspoon salt
½ teaspoon cinnamon
2 teaspoons achiote chili powder
1 tablespoon unsweetened cocoa powder
¼ cup cinnamon
½ cup confectioners' sugar
¼ cup tapioca flour
Oil spray
1 cup granulated sugar

Continued on page 70

Continue to whip until the mixture becomes very thick and is lukewarm, approximately 12 to 15 minutes. Add ½ teaspoon cinnamon and all of the achiote and cocoa powder during the last minute of whipping. While the mixture is whipping prepare the pan as follows.

Combine the confectioners' sugar and tapioca flour in a small bowl. Lightly spray a 9 × 9–inch metal baking pan with nonstick cooking spray. Add all the sugar and tapioca mixture and move around to completely coat the bottom and sides of the pan. Then mix the ¼ cup cinnamon and 1 cup granulated sugar in a small bowl, combining the two, and sprinkle some on the bottom of the 9 × 9–inch pan and set aside.

When ready, pour marshmallow into pan using a lightly oiled spatula. Lightly sprinkle some cinnamon sugar mixture and dust the top. Reserve the rest for later. Allow the marshmallows to sit uncovered for at least 6 hours and up to overnight.

Turn the marshmallows out onto a cutting board and cut into 1½–inch squares using a pizza wheel coated with cooking spray. Once cut, lightly dust all sides of each marshmallow with the remaining mixture of cinnamon sugar, using additional if necessary. Store in an airtight container for up to 3 weeks.

CHAPTER 5
Getting Fancy Mallows

TOASTED COCONUT

Place the gelatin into the bowl of a stand mixer along with ½ cup of cold water, and mix lightly to incorporate the water and gelatin. Have the whisk attachment standing by.

In a small metal or ceramic bowl, preferably not plastic, mix two egg whites till they are stiff peaks and set aside.

In a small saucepan, combine ½ cup water at room temperature, sugar, simple syrup or light corn syrup, and salt. Place over medium-high heat, clip a candy thermometer (best to use a digital thermometer if you have one) onto the side of the pan, and continue to cook until the mixture reaches 240°F, approximately 7 to 8 minutes. Once the mixture reaches this temperature, immediately remove from the heat.

Turn the mixer on low speed and, while running, slowly pour the sugar syrup down the side of the bowl into the gelatin mixture. Once you have added all the syrup, increase the speed to medium and mix until gelatin is dissolved. Once dissolved, turn off mixer and add in egg whites. Turn mixer to high.

1¼ ounces kosher gelatin
½ cup cold water
2 large egg whites
½ cup room-temperature water
2 cups pure cane sugar
½ cup simple syrup or light corn syrup
¼ teaspoon salt
1 tablespoon coconut emulsion
½ cup confectioners' sugar
¼ cup tapioca flour
Oil spray
2 cups toasted coconut

Continued on page 76

Continue to whip until the mixture becomes very thick and is lukewarm, approximately 12 to 15 minutes. Add the coconut emulsion during the last minute of whipping. While the mixture is whipping, prepare the pan as follows.

Combine the confectioners' sugar and tapioca flour in a small bowl. Lightly spray a 9 × 9–inch metal baking pan with nonstick cooking spray. Add the sugar and tapioca mixture and move around to completely coat the bottom and sides of the pan. Then sprinkle the bottom of the pan with some of the crushed toasted coconut.

When ready, using a lightly oiled spatula, pour marshmallow into the pan. Sprinkle more of the toasted coconut on top, and reserve the rest for later. Allow the marshmallows to sit uncovered for at least 6 hours and up to overnight.

Turn the marshmallows out onto a cutting board and cut into 1½–inch squares using a pizza wheel coated with cooking spray. Once cut, lightly dust all sides of each marshmallow with the remaining toasted coconut, using additional if necessary. Store in an airtight container for up to 3 weeks.

COFFEE MOCHA

Place the gelatin into the bowl of a stand mixer along with ½ cup of cold dark roast coffee; mix lightly to incorporate the coffee and gelatin. Have the whisk attachment standing by.

In a small metal or ceramic bowl, preferably not plastic, mix two egg whites till they are stiff peaks and set aside.

In a small saucepan, combine ½ cup water at room temperature, sugar, simple syrup or light corn syrup, and salt. Place over medium-high heat, clip a candy thermometer (best to use a digital thermometer if you have one) onto the side of the pan, and continue to cook until the mixture reaches 240°F, approximately 7 to 8 minutes. Once the mixture reaches this temperature, immediately remove from the heat.

Turn the mixer on low speed and, while running, slowly pour the sugar syrup down the side of the bowl into the gelatin mixture. Once you have added all of the syrup, increase the speed to medium and mix until gelatin is dissolved. Once dissolved, turn off mixer and add in egg whites. Turn mixer to high.

- 1¼ ounces of kosher gelatin
- ½ cup cold dark roast coffee
- 2 large egg whites
- ½ cup room-temperature water
- 2 cups pure cane sugar
- ½ cup simple syrup or light corn syrup
- ¼ teaspoon salt
- 1 tablespoon cocoa powder
- Oil spray
- 1 cup powdered sugar
- ½ cup tapioca flour

Continued on page 78

Continue to whip until the mixture becomes very thick and is lukewarm, approximately 12 to 15 minutes. Add the cocoa powder during the last minute of whipping. While the mixture is whipping, prepare the pan as follows.

Combine the confectioners' sugar and tapioca flour in a small bowl. Lightly spray a 9 × 9–inch metal baking pan with nonstick cooking spray. Add some sugar and tapioca mixture and move around to completely coat the bottom and sides of the pan.

When ready, pour using a lightly oiled spatula. Once the marshmallow is evenly spread, dust the top with some confectioners' sugar and tapioca flour to coat. Reserve the rest for later. Allow the marshmallows to sit uncovered for at least 6 hours and up to overnight.

Turn the marshmallows out onto a cutting board and cut into 1½–inch squares using a pizza wheel coated with cooking spray. Once cut, lightly dust all sides of each marshmallow with the remaining mixture of confectioners' sugar and tapioca flour, using additional if necessary. Store in an airtight container for up to 3 weeks.

When we started this business, our families were very loving and supportive. Some were a little scared because we no longer had the security of an everyday paycheck or health insurance, but they knew it was something we had to do. My mother-in-law is from Costa Rica and the culture there believes in Pura Vida, which means remaining optimistic despite unfortunate circumstances. No worries, no fuss, no stress—Pura Vida. We believe in this daily in life and in our business, so it only made sense to get our morning coffee from Costa Rica. When I make our Coffee Mocha Marshmallows I use the coffee that we get from Costa Rica. My in-laws visited a few coffee plantations and sent us a box of amazing coffee in different roasts, and we chose one that was smooth and perfect for our marshmallows. Our marshmallows are Pura Vida, and making them set me on a course for a better life.

MINT CHOCOLATE CHIP

Place the gelatin into the bowl of a stand mixer along with ½ cup of cold water, and mix lightly to incorporate the water and gelatin. Have the whisk attachment standing by.

In a small metal or ceramic bowl, preferably not plastic, mix two egg whites till they are stiff peaks and set aside.

In a small saucepan combine ½ cup water at room temperature, sugar, simple syrup or light corn syrup, and salt. Place over medium-high heat, clip a candy thermometer (best to use a digital thermometer if you have one) onto the side of the pan, and continue to cook until the mixture reaches 240°F, approximately 7 to 8 minutes. Once the mixture reaches this temperature, immediately remove from the heat.

Turn the mixer on low speed and, while running, slowly pour the sugar syrup down the side of the bowl into the gelatin mixture. Once you have added all the syrup, increase the speed to medium and mix until gelatin is dissolved. Once dissolved, turn off mixer and add in egg whites. Turn mixer to high.

Continue to whip until the mixture becomes very thick and is lukewarm,

1¼ ounces kosher gelatin
½ cup cold water
2 large egg whites
½ cup room-temperature water
2 cups pure cane sugar
½ cup simple syrup or light corn syrup
¼ teaspoon salt
1 teaspoon mint chocolate extract
2 drops green food gel color
1 cup mini chocolate chips
1 cup confectioners' sugar
½ cup tapioca flour
Oil spray

Continued on page 82

approximately 12 to 15 minutes. Add the extract and food coloring during the last minute of whipping. While the mixture is whipping, prepare the pan as follows.

Combine the confectioners' sugar and tapioca flour in a small bowl. Lightly spray a 9 × 9–inch metal baking pan with nonstick cooking spray. Add some sugar and tapioca mixture and move around to completely coat the bottom and sides of the pan.

When ready, before pouring the marshmallow mixture into the prepared pan, sprinkle ¼ cup of chocolate chips into the marshmallow. Fold lightly and pour half using a lightly oiled spatula to spread evenly into the pan. With the other half of the marshmallow,

repeat the above, sprinkling the remaining chocolate chips and folding before pouring the rest into the pan. Once the marshmallow is evenly spread, dust the top with some of the confectioners' sugar and tapioca flour mixture. Reserve the rest for later. Allow the marshmallows to sit uncovered for at least 6 hours and up to overnight.

Turn the marshmallows out onto a cutting board and cut into 1½–inch squares using a pizza wheel coated with cooking spray. Once cut, lightly dust all sides of each marshmallow with the remaining mixture of confectioners' sugar and tapioca flour, using additional if necessary. Store in an airtight container for up to 3 weeks.

CHURRO

Place the gelatin into the bowl of a stand mixer along with ½ cup of cold water, and mix lightly to incorporate the water and gelatin. Have the whisk attachment standing by.

In a small metal or ceramic bowl, preferably not plastic, mix two egg whites till they are stiff peaks and set aside.

In a small saucepan, combine ½ cup water at room temperature, 2 cups sugar, simple syrup or light corn syrup, and salt. Place over medium-high heat, clip a candy thermometer (best to use a digital thermometer if you have one) onto the side of the pan, and continue to cook until the mixture reaches 240°F, approximately 7 to 8 minutes. Once the mixture reaches this temperature, immediately remove from the heat.

Turn the mixer on low speed and, while running, slowly pour the sugar syrup down the side of the bowl into the gelatin mixture. Once you have added all of the syrup, increase the speed to medium and mix until gelatin is dissolved. Once dissolved, turn off mixer and add in egg whites. Turn mixer to high.

1¼ ounces kosher gelatin
½ cup cold water
2 large egg whites
½ cup room-temperature water
3 cups pure cane sugar
½ cup simple syrup or light corn syrup
¼ teaspoon salt
1 teaspoon cinnamon
1 cup confectioners' sugar
½ cup tapioca flour
¼ cup cinnamon
Oil spray

Continued on page 84

Continue to whip until the mixture becomes very thick and is lukewarm, approximately 12 to 15 minutes. Add 1 teaspoon cinnamon during the last minute of whipping. While the mixture is whipping, prepare the pan as follows.

Combine the confectioners' sugar and tapioca flour in a small bowl. Lightly spray a 9 × 9–inch metal baking pan with nonstick cooking spray. Add some sugar and tapioca mixture and move around to completely coat the bottom and sides of the pan. Then combine the ¼ cup cinnamon and 1 cup sugar. Lightly sprinkle some on the bottom of the baking pan and place the remaining to the side.

When ready, pour marshmallow into baking pan using a lightly oiled spatula. Once the marshmallow is evenly spread, dust the top with some of the cinnamon sugar. Reserve the rest for later. Allow the marshmallows to sit uncovered for at least 6 hours and up to overnight.

Turn the marshmallows out onto a cutting board and cut into 1½–inch squares using a pizza wheel coated with cooking spray. Once cut, lightly dust all sides of each marshmallow with the remaining mixture of cinnamon sugar, using additional if necessary. Store in an airtight container for up to 3 weeks.

I created these marshmallows because of my love for the churros at Disneyland. First thing we do when we visit is find the closest churro stand and get one. Then, throughout the day we'd get more. So, I wanted to create a marsh-mallow that reminded me of that and would remind others of the same experience. Not only can you eat these delicious marshmallows straight after cutting, but you can cut them down to plop into your coffee or hot cocoa to give your drink that authentic churro taste.

PEANUT BUTTER

Place the gelatin into the bowl of a stand mixer along with ½ cup of cold water, and mix lightly to incorporate the water and gelatin. Have the whisk attachment standing by.

In a small metal or ceramic bowl, preferably not plastic, mix two egg whites till they are stiff peaks and set aside.

In a small saucepan, combine ½ cup water at room temperature, sugar, simple syrup or light corn syrup, and salt. Place over medium-high heat, clip a candy thermometer (best to use a digital thermometer if you have one) onto the side of the pan, and continue to cook until the mixture reaches 240°F, approximately 7 to 8 minutes. Once the mixture reaches this temperature, immediately remove from the heat.

Turn the mixer on low speed and, while running, slowly pour the sugar syrup down the side of the bowl into the gelatin mixture. Once you have added all of the syrup, increase the speed to medium and mix until gelatin is dissolved. Once dissolved, turn off mixer and add in egg whites. Turn mixer to high.

- 1¼ ounces kosher gelatin
- ½ cup cold water
- 2 large egg whites
- ½ cup room-temperature water
- 3 cups pure cane sugar
- ½ cup simple syrup or light corn syrup
- ¼ teaspoon salt
- 1 cup confectioners' sugar
- ½ cup tapioca flour
- Oil spray
- 2 tablespoons peanut butter, smooth or chunky

Continued on page 88

Continue to whip until the mixture becomes very thick and is lukewarm, approximately 12 to 15 minutes. While the mixture is whipping, prepare the pan as follows.

Combine the confectioners' sugar and tapioca flour in a small bowl. Lightly spray a 9 × 9–inch metal baking pan with nonstick cooking spray. Add some sugar and tapioca mixture and move around to completely coat the bottom and sides of the pan.

When ready, scoop a quarter of the marshmallow into a mixing bowl and add the 2 tablespoons of peanut butter. Combine the mixture thoroughly, and place half of the peanut butter mixture into the rest of the marshmallow. Fold using a lightly oiled spatula—do not overmix—and then pour half into the pan. Repeat this process with the remainder of the peanut butter mix and marshmallow. Once the marshmallow is evenly spread, dust the top with some of the confectioners' sugar and tapioca flour. Reserve the rest for later. Allow the marshmallows to sit uncovered for at least 6 hours and up to overnight.

Turn the marshmallows out onto a cutting board and cut into 1½–inch squares using a pizza wheel coated with cooking spray. Once cut, lightly dust all sides of each marshmallow with the remaining mixture of confectioners' sugar and tapioca flour, using additional if necessary. Store in an airtight container for up to 3 weeks.

When I started making the peanut butter marshmallows, I used your general store brand peanut butter, but when I started my small business, I started to recognize other small businesses, too. I noticed a young man who made his own all natural peanut butter—nothing more than peanuts and sea salt. Being an entrepreneur and owning your own business, you realize and know how much time and work goes into building your craft and brand. As a small business and a beginning entrepreneur, I knew I needed to support locally. I remember meeting Jeff Malkoon, owner of Peanut Butter Americano, and seeing how proud he was of his craft and what he was doing. I told him what I was doing and how I started and that I was interested in trying his peanut butter in my marshmallows. He handed me a jar and told me to try it, free of charge, and with his smile and trust, I did just that. Three years in, making marshmallows at my retail location, I still use his all-natural peanut butter because I believe in helping other small business and entrepreneurs and because it tastes that much better. Store-bought peanut butter has sugar and other additives and, again, marshmallows are absorbent to ingredients and flavors. Now my marshmallows are not saturated with extra sugar and oils, and I can tell people that my peanut butter marshmallow is all natural.

CHAPTER 6

Dipped Mallows

CARAMEL PEANUT

Place the gelatin into the bowl of a stand mixer along with ½ cup of cold water, and mix lightly to incorporate the water and gelatin. Have the whisk attachment standing by.

In a small metal or ceramic bowl, preferably not plastic, mix two egg whites till they are stiff peaks and set aside.

In a small saucepan, combine ½ cup water at room temperature, sugar, simple syrup or light corn syrup, and salt. Place over medium-high heat, clip a candy thermometer (best to use a digital thermometer if you have one) onto the side of the pan, and continue to cook until the mixture reaches 240°F, approximately 7 to 8 minutes. Once the mixture reaches this temperature, immediately remove from the heat.

Turn the mixer on low speed and, while running, slowly pour the sugar syrup down the side of the bowl into the gelatin mixture. Once you have added all of the syrup, increase the speed to medium and mix until gelatin is dissolved. Once dissolved, turn off mixer and add in egg whites. Turn mixer to high.

1¼ ounces of kosher gelatin
½ cup cold water
2 large egg whites
½ cup room-temperature water
2 cups pure cane sugar
½ cup simple syrup or light corn syrup
¼ teaspoon salt
1 teaspoon vanilla bean paste
1 cup confectioners' sugar
½ cup tapioca flour
1 cup chopped peanuts
1 cup caramel bits
Oil spray
2 cups milk chocolate candy wafers
Crushed peanuts, for garnish

Continued on page 94

Continue to whip until the mixture becomes very thick and is lukewarm, approximately 12 to 15 minutes. Add the vanilla bean paste during the last minute of whipping. While the mixture is whipping, prepare the pan as follows.

Combine the confectioners' sugar and tapioca flour in a small bowl. Lightly spray a 9 × 9–inch metal baking pan with nonstick cooking spray. Add some sugar and tapioca mixture and move around to completely coat the bottom and sides of the pan. Add the caramel bits to a food processor and grind them fine.

When ready, before pouring the marshmallow mixture into the prepared pan, sprinkle some of the peanuts and the caramel bits on top of the marshmallow. Fold lightly and pour half using a lightly oiled spatula into the pan. With the other half of the marshmallow, sprinkle the remaining peanuts and handful of caramel bits; lightly fold and pour the rest into the pan. Once the marshmallow is evenly spread, dust the top with some confectioners' sugar and tapioca flour. Reserve the rest for later. Allow the marshmallows to sit uncovered for at least 6 hours and up to overnight.

Turn the marshmallows out onto a cutting board and cut into 1½–inch squares using a pizza wheel coated with cooking spray. Once cut, lightly dust all sides of each marshmallow with the remaining mixture of confectioners' sugar and tapioca flour, using additional if necessary.

Melt the milk chocolate candy wafers in a small microwave-safe bowl or double boiler. Once melted, take marshmallows one at a time and dip halfway into the chocolate. Place marshmallow on a parchment paper and top with crushed peanuts. Now you have your very own marshmallow Snickers bar.

ORANGE CREAM

After following the recipe on making a classic Vanilla Bean Marshmallow on page 19, turn the marshmallows out onto a cutting board and cut into 1½–inch squares using a pizza wheel coated with cooking spray. Once cut, lightly dust all sides of each marshmallow with the remaining mixture of confectioners' sugar and tapioca flour from that recipe, using additional if necessary.

Melt the orange wafers in a microwave-safe bowl and, once melted, place the orange oil in the chocolate and mix. Once combined, dip the vanilla marshmallows into the chocolate halfway and place on parchment paper. Before the chocolate dries, sprinkle the white nonpareils on top. Once dried, you have your very own Creamsicle, or as my grandmother would have called it, a 50/50 bar.

Vanilla Bean Marshmallows (see page 19)
1 cup orange colored chocolate wafers
1 teaspoon orange oil
white nonpareils

S'MORES

Place the gelatin into the bowl of a stand mixer along with ½ cup of cold water, and mix lightly to incorporate the water and gelatin. Have the whisk attachment standing by.

In a small stainless steel or ceramic bowl, preferably not plastic, mix two egg whites till they are stiff peaks and set aside.

In a small saucepan, combine ½ cup water at room temperature, simple syrup or light corn syrup, sugar, and salt. Place over medium high heat, clip a candy thermometer (best to use a digital thermometer if you have one) onto the side of the pan, and continue to cook until the mixture reaches 240°F, approximately 7 to 8 minutes. Once the mixture reaches this temperature, immediately remove from the heat.

Turn the mixer on low speed and, while running, slowly pour the sugar syrup down the side of the bowl into the gelatin mixture. Once you have added all the syrup, increase the speed to medium and mix until gelatin is dissolved. Once dissolved, turn off mixer and add in egg whites. Turn mixer to high.

1¼ ounces kosher gelatin
½ cup cold water
2 large egg whites
½ cup room-temperature water
½ cup simple syrup or light corn syrup
2 cups pure cane sugar
¼ teaspoon salt
1 teaspoon vanilla bean paste
1 tablespoon cocoa powder
½ cup confectioners' sugar
¼ cup tapioca flour
Oil spray
2 cups graham cracker crumbs
2 cups milk chocolate wafers

Note: You will need two mixers for this marshmallow, and don't forget your 9 × 9-inch pan!

Continued on page 100

Once eggs have been added, let mix for five minutes. You don't want this marshmallow to get too firm since you must divide between two mixers. After five minutes, pour half of the marshmallow mix into the second mixer and turn both mixers to medium speed.

Continue to whip until the mixture becomes very thick and is lukewarm, approximately 10 minutes. In that last minute, in one mixer you will add the vanilla bean paste, and in the second mixer, you will add the cocoa powder, and then continue mixing. While the mixture is whipping, prepare the pan as follows.

Combine the confectioners' sugar and tapioca flour in a small bowl. Lightly spray a 9 × 9–inch metal baking pan with nonstick cooking spray. Add some sugar and tapioca mixture and move around to completely coat the bottom and sides of the pan. Then sprinkle an even layer of graham cracker crumbs on the bottom of the pan.

When ready, pour the vanilla bean marshmallow mixture using a lightly oiled spatula, which is used for spreading the marshmallow evenly into the pan. Once spread, take the chocolate marshmallow and pour over the vanilla flavor. Dust the top with enough of the remaining graham cracker crumbs to lightly cover. Reserve the rest for later. Allow the marshmallows to sit uncovered for at least 6 hours and up to overnight.

Turn the marshmallows out onto a cutting board and cut into 1½–inch squares using a pizza wheel coated with cooking spray. Once cut, lightly dust all sides of each marshmallow with the graham cracker.

Once the mashmallows are cut and dusted, you'll want to melt some milk chocolate candy melts in a small microwave-safe bowl or double boiler. Once chocolate melts, dip each marshmallow on its side, so half the chocolate and half the vanilla get coated with the melted milk chocolate. Place dipped marshmallows on parchment paper and sprinkle graham cracker on top—instant s'more without the fire.

This marshmallow is more difficult in the making, but very much worth it when done. This is one s'more that does not need a fire and can be enjoyed as a dessert. This marshmallow is one of our top sellers in our retail location and enjoyed by many.

ROCKY ROAD

Place the gelatin into the bowl of a stand mixer along with ½ cup of cold water, and mix lightly to incorporate the water and gelatin. Have the whisk attachment standing by.

In a small metal or ceramic bowl, preferably not plastic, mix two egg whites till they are stiff peaks and set aside.

In a small saucepan, combine ½ cup water at room temperature, sugar, simple syrup or light corn syrup, and salt. Place over medium-high heat, clip a candy thermometer (best to use a digital thermometer if you have one) onto the side of the pan, and continue to cook until the mixture reaches 240°F, approximately 7 to 8 minutes. Once the mixture reaches this temperature, immediately remove from the heat.

Turn the mixer on low speed and, while running, slowly pour the sugar syrup down the side of the bowl into the gelatin mixture. Once you have added all of the syrup, increase the speed to medium and mix until gelatin is dissolved. Once dissolved, turn off mixer and add in egg whites. Turn mixer to high.

Continue to whip until the mixture becomes very thick and is lukewarm, approximately 12 to 15 minutes. Add the vanilla bean paste during the last minute

1¼ ounces kosher gelatin
½ cup cold water
2 large egg whites
½ cup room-temperature water
2 cups pure cane sugar
½ cup simple syrup or light corn syrup
¼ teaspoon salt
1 teaspoon vanilla bean paste
1 cup confectioners' sugar
½ cup tapioca flour
2 cups milk chocolate wafers
Oil spray
1 cup chopped walnuts

Continued on page 104

of whipping. While the mixture is whipping, prepare the pan as follows.

Combine the confectioners' sugar and tapioca flour in a small bowl. Lightly spray a 9 × 9–inch metal baking pan with nonstick cooking spray. Add some sugar and tapioca mixture and move around to completely coat the bottom and sides of the pan.

When ready, sprinkle ½ cup of the chopped walnuts and fold into the marshmallow. Pour the marshmallow mixture into the prepared pan using a lightly oiled spatula for spreading evenly into the pan. Dust the top with some of the confectioners' sugar and tapioca flour. Reserve the rest for later. Allow the marshmallows to sit uncovered for at least 6 hours and up to overnight.

Turn the marshmallows out onto a cutting board and cut into 1½–inch squares using a pizza wheel coated with cooking spray. Once cut, lightly dust all sides of each marshmallow with the remaining mixture of confectioners' sugar and tapioca flour, using additional if necessary.

Place the parchment paper on a flat surface, and melt the milk chocolate wafers in a microwave-safe bowl or double boiler. Dip half of a marshmallow into the chocolate and place on parchment paper. Place a couple of the remaining crushed walnut pieces on top of the chocolate and let dry. Repeat with remaining marshmallows.

M&M

Place the gelatin into the bowl of a stand mixer along with ½ cup of cold water, and mix lightly to incorporate the water and gelatin. Have the whisk attachment standing by.

In a small metal or ceramic bowl, preferably not plastic, mix two egg whites till they are stiff peaks and set aside.

In a small saucepan, combine ½ cup water at room temperature, sugar, simple syrup or light corn syrup, and salt. Place over medium-high heat, clip a candy thermometer (best to use a digital thermometer if you have one) onto the side of the pan, and continue to cook until the mixture reaches 240°F, approximately 7 to 8 minutes. Once the mixture reaches this temperature, immediately remove from the heat.

Turn the mixer on low speed and, while running, slowly pour the sugar syrup down the side of the bowl into the gelatin mixture. Once you have added all of the syrup, increase the speed to medium and mix until gelatin is dissolved. Once dissolved, turn off mixer and add in egg whites. Turn mixer to high.

Continue to whip until the mixture becomes very thick and is lukewarm,

1¼ ounces kosher gelatin
½ cup cold water
2 large egg whites
½ cup room-temperature water
2 cups pure cane sugar
½ cup simple syrup or light corn syrup
¼ teaspoon salt
1 teaspoon vanilla bean paste
1 cup confectioners' sugar
½ cup tapioca flour
1 cup mini M&M's
Oil spray
2 cups milk chocolate wafers
2 cups mini M&M's

Continued on page 106

approximately 12 to 15 minutes. Add the vanilla bean paste during the last minute of whipping. While the mixture is whipping, prepare the pan as follows.

Combine the confectioners' sugar and tapioca flour in a small bowl. Lightly spray a 9 × 9–inch metal baking pan with nonstick cooking spray. Add some of the sugar and tapioca mixture and move around to completely coat the bottom and sides of the pan.

When ready, before pouring the marshmallow mixture into the prepared pan, fold in a cup of the mini M&M's. and, using a lightly oiled spatula to spread evenly into the pan. Dust the top with enough of the confectioners' sugar and tapioca flour to cover. Reserve the rest for later. Allow the marshmallows to sit uncovered for at least 6 hours and up to overnight.

Turn the marshmallows out onto a cutting board and cut into 1½–inch squares using a pizza wheel coated with cooking spray. Once cut, lightly dust all sides of each marshmallow with the remaining mixture of confectioners' sugar and tapioca flour, using additional if necessary.

Place parchment paper on a flat surface, and melt milk chocolate wafers in a microwave-safe bowl. Melt in 20-second increments so not to burn the chocolate, and stir in between till smooth and ready for dipping. Once melted, dip half of each marshmallow into the melted milk chocolate and top with mini M&M's.

SALTED CARAMEL

Prepare the Vanilla Bean Marshmallows as stated on pages 19–20. Combine the confectioners' sugar and tapioca flour in a small bowl. Lightly spray a 9 × 9–inch metal baking pan with nonstick cooking spray. Add some sugar and tapioca mixture and move around to completely coat the bottom and sides of the pan.

Melt the caramel in a microwave-safe bowl for 20-second increments till runny, making sure not to burn it. Once it is melted, mix in the ½ teaspoon sea salt and combine thoroughly. Taste it to make sure you have achieved that sweet and salty taste.

When ready, dip your spatula into the caramel and fold it into half of your marshmallow mixture. Do not overmix because you will lose the ribbon effect the caramel gives the marshmallow. Pour the marshmallow mixture into the prepared pan, using a lightly oiled spatula for spreading evenly into the pan. Dust the top with some of the confectioners' sugar and tapioca flour. Reserve the rest for later. Allow the marshmallows to sit uncovered for at least 6 hours and up to overnight.

Vanilla Bean Marshmallows
  (see on page 19)
1 cup confectioners' sugar
½ cup tapioca flour
Oil spray
1 cup caramel
½ teaspoon sea salt
2 cups dark chocolate
  wafers
¼ cup sea salt

Continued on page 110

Turn the marshmallows out onto a cutting board and cut into 1½–inch squares using a pizza wheel coated with cooking spray. Once cut, lightly dust all sides of each marshmallow with the remaining mixture of confectioners' sugar and tapioca flour, using additional if necessary.

Place parchment paper on a flat surface and melt your dark chocolate wafers in a microwave-safe bowl. Melt these in 20-second increments to ensure the chocolate does not burn and then stir till smooth.

Once melted, dip each marshmallow halfway and place on parchment to dry. Before the chocolate dries, sprinkle a few grains of sea salt on top.

CHAPTER 7
Extras

MARSHMALLOW WHIP

This recipe will make 3 16-ounce jars of marshmallow whip.

Place the egg whites into the bowl of a stand mixer along with the cream of tartar, and mix on medium till firm peaks form.

In a small saucepan, combine water, sugar, and simple syrup or light corn syrup. Place over medium-high heat, clip a candy thermometer (best to use a digital thermometer if you have one) onto the side of the pan, and continue to cook until the mixture reaches 240°F, approximately 7 to 8 minutes. Once the mixture reaches this temperature, immediately remove from the heat.

Turn the mixer on low speed and, while running, slowly pour the sugar syrup down the side of the bowl into the egg whites. Make sure this is poured slowly; if poured too fast, you could cook the egg whites. Once you have added all the syrup, increase the speed to medium.

Continue to whip until the mixture becomes very thick and glossy, approximately 10 to 12 minutes. Add the vanilla bean paste during the last minute of whipping.

When ready, pour the marshmallow mixture into a container to use at your leisure. You can store this in your refrigerator for up to 2 weeks, if it lasts that long.

3 large egg whites
1 teaspoon cream of tartar
⅓ cup water
¾ cup of sugar
¾ cup simple syrup or light corn syrup
1 teaspoon vanilla bean paste

HOMEMADE GRAHAM CRACKERS

Preheat oven to 350°F.

Place all dry ingredients into the bowl of a stand mixer and mix until well blended. Add in the butter and allow the mix to blend thoroughly until the dough resembles bread crumbs.

Turn off mixer and add in all the wet ingredients—water, honey, and molasses. Mix these ingredients until the dough becomes a little sticky and pliable.

Once dough is complete, place it on a floured surface and roll out to ¼ inch, make sure to flour your rolling pin so it does not stick to the dough. (A trick is to roll the dough between two pieces of parchment paper.)

Once rolled out, you can use your favorite cookie cutter to cut out shapes that you will enjoy for your homemade s'mores.

Bake these for 10 minutes or until the edges brown. Serve with your favorite mallows!

3 cups all-purpose flour
2 cups wheat flour
1 cup brown sugar
1 teaspoon salt
2 teaspoons cinnamon
2 teaspoons baking soda
1 cup cubed cold butter
½ cup water
½ cup honey
2 tablespoons molasses

VANILLA MALLOW PIES

This recipe will make 23 mallow pies.

You will want to make the graham crackers ahead of time for this recipe, and use a 3-inch circle cookie cut out. Once you have baked all your cookies then move on to the marshmallow mix for your mallow pies.

Place the gelatin into the bowl of a stand mixer along with ½ cup of cold water, and mix lightly to incorporate the water and gelatin. Have the whisk attachment standing by.

In a small metal or ceramic bowl, preferably not plastic, mix 3 egg whites till they are stiff peaks and set aside.

In a small saucepan, combine ¼ cup water at room temperature, sugar, honey, and simple syrup or light corn syrup. Place over medium-high heat, clip a candy thermometer (best to use a digital thermometer if you have one) onto the side of the pan, and continue to cook until the mixture reaches 240°F, approximately 7 to 8 minutes. Once the mixture reaches this temperature, immediately remove from the heat.

Graham Cracker recipe on page 115
4 teaspoons kosher gelatin
½ cup water ice cold
3 large egg whites
¼ cup room-temperature water
¾ cup granulated sugar
3 tablespoons honey (clover or wildflower)
4 tablespoons simple syrup or light corn syrup
1 teaspoon vanilla bean paste
4 cups milk chocolate wafers

Continued on page 118

Turn the mixer on low speed and, while running, slowly pour the sugar syrup down the side of the bowl into the gelatin mixture. Once you have added all of the syrup, increase the speed to medium and mix until gelatin is dissolved. Once dissolved, turn off mixer and add in egg whites. Turn mixer to high.

Continue to whip until the mixture becomes thick and is lukewarm, approximately 12 to 15 minutes. Add the 1 teaspoon vanilla bean paste during the last minute of whipping.

Arrange your cookies before mixture is done. After marshmallow mixture is done, you must work quickly since marshmallow sets up fast. Fill a piping bag halfway with the marshmallow mixture, and pipe onto a cookie in a beehive motion. After piping minimum of 5, gently place a second cookie on top and slightly press. Repeat this process till you have run out of cookies or marshmallow.

Set up a double broiler (a medium saucepan filled with water and metal bowl that sits above it); place the chocolate wafers in the bowl. Set the bowl on top of the saucepan and boil over medium heat. This will melt the chocolate evenly. Make sure to stir occasionally so that the chocolate does not burn.

Once the chocolate is melted, remove it from the heat and place parchment paper on a flat surface. Place a cookie sandwich into the chocolate and completely submerge it. Using a fork, lift it out of the chocolate and lightly shake off any excess chocolate. Place it on the parchment paper to cool and enjoy.

These must be my favorite marsh-mallow dessert to create. When I worked retail, we had Moon Pies stocked, and every day my break-fast consisted of a Moon Pie. Once I opened my store location, I wanted to re-create this delicious treat and so, with trial and error and a lot of taste testing, we came up with this one. I know in the recipe it says chocolate wafers, which is cost effective, but if you can find really good chocolate that will harden up, then I would suggest you do so. It will make a world of difference.

CUTOUT POPS

Make the Vanilla Bean Marshmallow recipe (page 19) but instead of pouring into a 9 x 9–inch pan, you'll want to pour it into a 9 x 13–inch cake pan to make a thinner marshmallow for cutouts.

Once the marshmallow has set, you can use any cookie cutters you'd like to cut out the shapes in the marshmallow. Make sure to use cooking spray on the cookie cutter so that the cutter does not stick to the marshmallow. You'll have to re-spray every third cutout because the marshmallow will start to stick and tear.

Once you have a cutout, you can roll it in any color sanding sugar you would like.

After this, melt your chocolate in a microwave-safe bowl in 15-second increment so that the chocolate doesn't burn. You will only need a little bit of the chocolate because you'll be dipping your straw or lollipop stick into it as a glue. Once you dip it into the chocolate, push it through the bottom of the marshmallow till it almost comes out the other side.

Let your cutout dry or decorate as you'd like.

Vanilla Bean Marshmallows
(recipe on page 19)
Oil spray
Sanding sugar
½ cup chocolate melts

Note: You'll need cookie cutters and fun straws or sticks for this recipe.

This is a fun activity for families or friends to enjoy. They can each make their own marshmallow pops for special occasions or just because they love mallows.

Acknowledgments

First, thank you to Nicole Frail at Skyhorse Publishing for finding me and helping me make this opportunity happen. I had just sent out a query to another publisher and was denied, so I'd thought I didn't have that niche to write about. It's true that when one door closes, two more open.

Thank you to the amazing and talented Joanie Simon who did all the awesome photography in the book. Her vision and ideas were just amazing. I let her run with the ideas and be one with the marshmallows, and the outcome was just brilliant. I'm so happy that our paths crossed.

Thank you to my customers. Without them, I wouldn't be able to bounce ideas around and see them come to life. They are brave to taste all my creations and encourage me to continue to think outside the box.

To my friends and family who have been supportive since I leaped off that ledge with no idea where I would land but they kept saying we could do it. On days I sat in the corner with my head down, your words of encouragement and willingness to help spread the word of my marshmallows encouraged us to keep moving forward. Our moms, dad, sisters, brothers, nieces, nephews, son, and daughter have at one point played a part in our marshmallow madness, and without them on some days, it wouldn't have been possible.

To my amazing wife—without you, this would still just be an idea, but you made it a reality. I could not think of one single person I'd rather ride this journey with. You inspire me, hold me, and encourage me daily. We have created something unique and I look forward to seeing this explode with you by my side. Thank you for being my Wonder Woman.

Finally, my grandmother—although you have passed, I know you are here with me. You would always ask "What would I do without you?" and thankfully you never had to find out. When you passed, I asked that same question of you, and you answered by giving me this, so thank you, Grandma, thank you for this.

Index

Conversion Charts

METRIC AND IMPERIAL CONVERSIONS

(These conversions are rounded for convenience)

Ingredient	Cups/Tablespoons/Teaspoons	Ounces	Grams/Milliliters
Butter	1 cup = 16 tablespoons = 2 sticks	8 ounces	230 grams
Cheese, shredded	1 cup	4 ounces	110 grams
Cream cheese	1 tablespoon	0.5 ounce	14.5 grams
Cornstarch	1 tablespoon	0.3 ounce	8 grams
Flour, all-purpose	1 cup/1 tablespoon	4.5 ounces/0.3 ounce	125 grams/8 grams
Flour, whole wheat	1 cup	4 ounces	120 grams
Fruit, dried	1 cup	4 ounces	120 grams
Fruits or veggies, chopped	1 cup	5 to 7 ounces	145 to 200 grams
Fruits or veggies, puréed	1 cup	8.5 ounces	245 grams
Honey, maple syrup, or corn syrup	1 tablespoon	.75 ounce	20 grams
Liquids: cream, milk, water, or juice	1 cup	8 fluid ounces	240 milliliters
Oats	1 cup	5.5 ounces	150 grams
Salt	1 teaspoon	0.2 ounce	6 grams
Spices: cinnamon, cloves, ginger, or nutmeg (ground)	1 teaspoon	0.2 ounce	5 milliliters
Sugar, brown, firmly packed	1 cup	7 ounces	200 grams
Sugar, white	1 cup/1 tablespoon	7 ounces/0.5 ounce	200 grams/12.5 grams
Vanilla extract	1 teaspoon	0.2 ounce	4 grams

OVEN TEMPERATURES

Fahrenheit	Celsius	Gas Mark
225°	110°	¼
250°	120°	½
275°	140°	1
300°	150°	2
325°	160°	3
350°	180°	4
375°	190°	5
400°	200°	6
425°	220°	7
450°	230°	8